GRAPHIC HISTORY

THE BATTLE OF
GETTYSBURG

by Michael Burgan

illustrated by Steve Erwin, Keith Williams,
and Charles Barnett III

Consultant:
James M. McPherson
Professor of History
Princeton University
Princeton, New Jersey

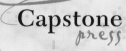

Capstone
press

Mankato, Minnesota

Graphic Library is published by Capstone Press,
151 Good Counsel Drive, P.O. Box 669, Mankato, Minnesota 56002.
www.capstonepress.com

Printed in the United States of America

1 2 3 4 5 6 11 10 09 08 07 06

Library of Congress Cataloging-in-Publication Data
Burgan, Michael.
The battle of Gettysburg / by Michael Burgan; illustrated by Steve Erwin, Keith Williams, and Charles Barnett III.
p. cm.—(Graphic library. Graphic history)
Summary: "In graphic novel format, tells the story of the Battle of Gettysburg, the three-day battle that was the turning point in the Civil War"—Provided by publisher.
Includes bibliographical references and index.
ISBN-13: 978-0-7368-5491-7 (hardcover)
ISBN-10: 0-7368-5491-6 (hardcover)
1. Gettysburg, Battle of, Gettysburg, Pa., 1863—Juvenile literature. I. Erwin, Steve, ill. II. Williams, Keith, 1958 Feb. 24– ill. III. Barnett, Charles, III, ill. IV. Title. V. Series.
E475.53.B965 2006
973.7'349—dc22 2005025380

Art Direction and Design
Bob Lentz

Production Artist
Alison Thiele

Colorist
Benjamin Hunzeker

Editor
Christine Peterson

Map on page 8 courtesy of the Geography and Map Division, Library of Congress.

Editor's note: Direct quotations from primary sources are indicated by a yellow background.

Direct quotations appear on the following pages:

Page 18, from General James Longstreet's account of the Battle of Gettysburg as published in the *Philadelphia Times* November 1876 (www.swcivilwar.com/LongstreetGettys1stPhilArticle.html).

Page 19, from George Pickett's letter dated July 4, 1863, as published in *Heart of a Soldier: As Revealed in the Intimate Letters of General George E. Pickett* (New York: S. Moyle, 1913).

Pages 20, 22, from *The Story of a Confederate Boy in the Civil War* by Virginia Infantryman David Emmons Johnston (Portland, Ore.: Glass & Prudhomme, 1914).

Page 23, from an article by Confederate Captain Robert A. Bright, originally published February 7, 1904, in the Richmond, Virginia, *Times-Dispatch*, and recorded in the Southern Historical Society Papers (http://docsouth.unc.edu/pickett/pickett.html#pick91).

Page 25, from a conversation between Abraham Lincoln and his secretary John Hay on July 14, 1863, as recorded in *Inside Lincoln's White House: The Complete Civil War Diary of John Hay* (Carbondale, Ill.: Southern Illinois University Press, 1997).

Pages 26, 29, from Abraham Lincoln's Gettysburg Address at the Library of Congress (http://www.loc.gov/exhibits/gadd/gadrft.html).

Table of Contents

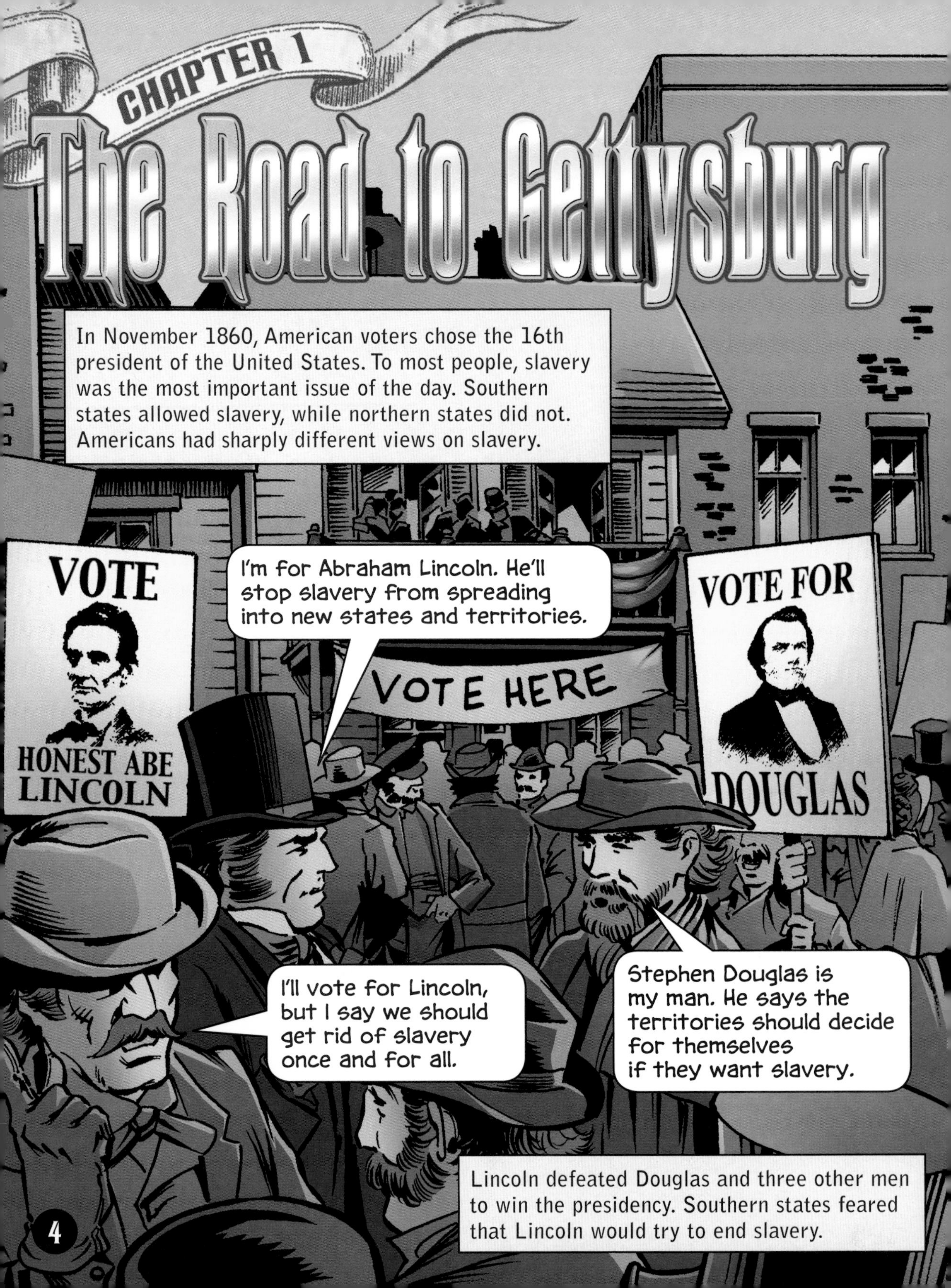
CHAPTER 1
The Road to Gettysburg
In November 1860, American voters chose the 16th president of the United States. To most people, slavery was the most important issue of the day. Southern states allowed slavery, while northern states did not. Americans had sharply different views on slavery.
VOTE
HONEST ABE LINCOLN
I'm for Abraham Lincoln. He'll stop slavery from spreading into new states and territories.
VOTE HERE
VOTE FOR
DOUGLAS
Stephen Douglas is my man. He says the territories should decide for themselves if they want slavery.
I'll vote for Lincoln, but I say we should get rid of slavery once and for all.
Lincoln defeated Douglas and three other men to win the presidency. Southern states feared that Lincoln would try to end slavery.

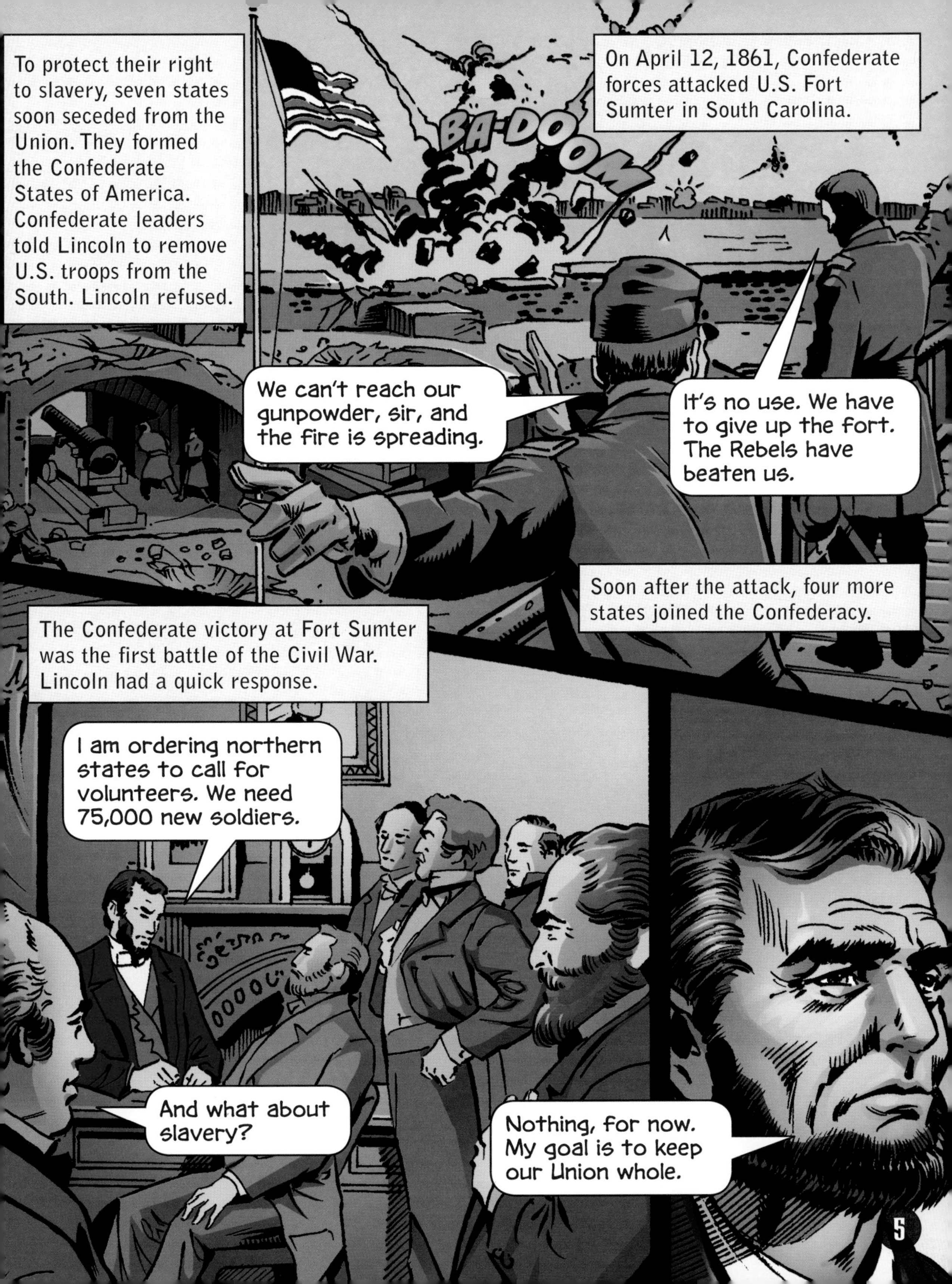
To protect their right to slavery, seven states soon seceded from the Union. They formed the Confederate States of America. Confederate leaders told Lincoln to remove U.S. troops from the South. Lincoln refused.
On April 12, 1861, Confederate forces attacked U.S. Fort Sumter in South Carolina.
BA-DOOM
We can't reach our gunpowder, sir, and the fire is spreading.
It's no use. We have to give up the fort. The Rebels have beaten us.
Soon after the attack, four more states joined the Confederacy.
The Confederate victory at Fort Sumter was the first battle of the Civil War. Lincoln had a quick response.
I am ordering northern states to call for volunteers. We need 75,000 new soldiers.
And what about slavery?
Nothing, for now. My goal is to keep our Union whole.

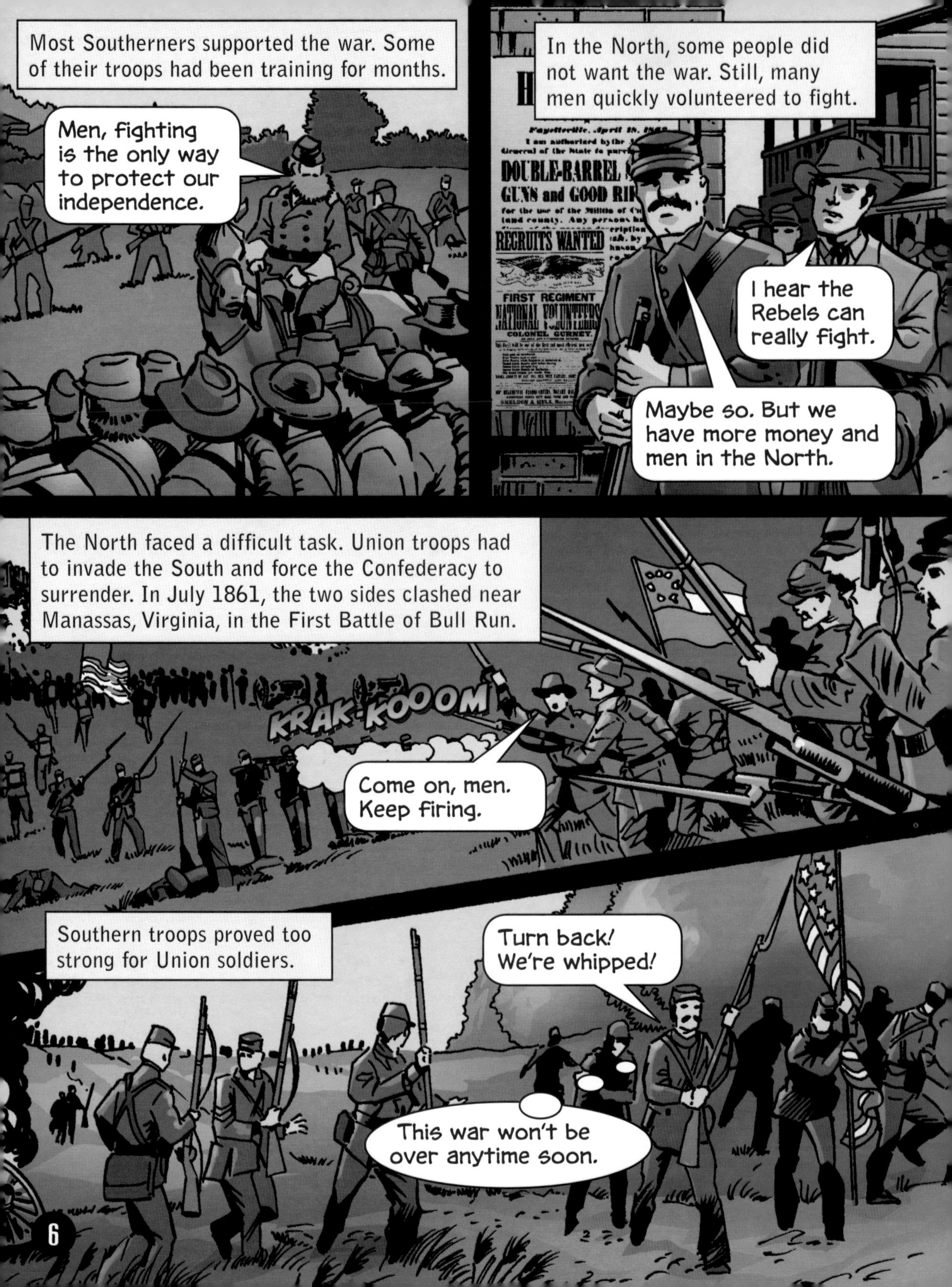
Most Southerners supported the war. Some of their troops had been training for months.
Men, fighting is the only way to protect our independence.
In the North, some people did not want the war. Still, many men quickly volunteered to fight.
I hear the Rebels can really fight.
Maybe so. But we have more money and men in the North.
The North faced a difficult task. Union troops had to invade the South and force the Confederacy to surrender. In July 1861, the two sides clashed near Manassas, Virginia, in the First Battle of Bull Run.
KRAK-KOOOM
Come on, men. Keep firing.
Southern troops proved too strong for Union soldiers.
Turn back! We're whipped!
This war won't be over anytime soon.

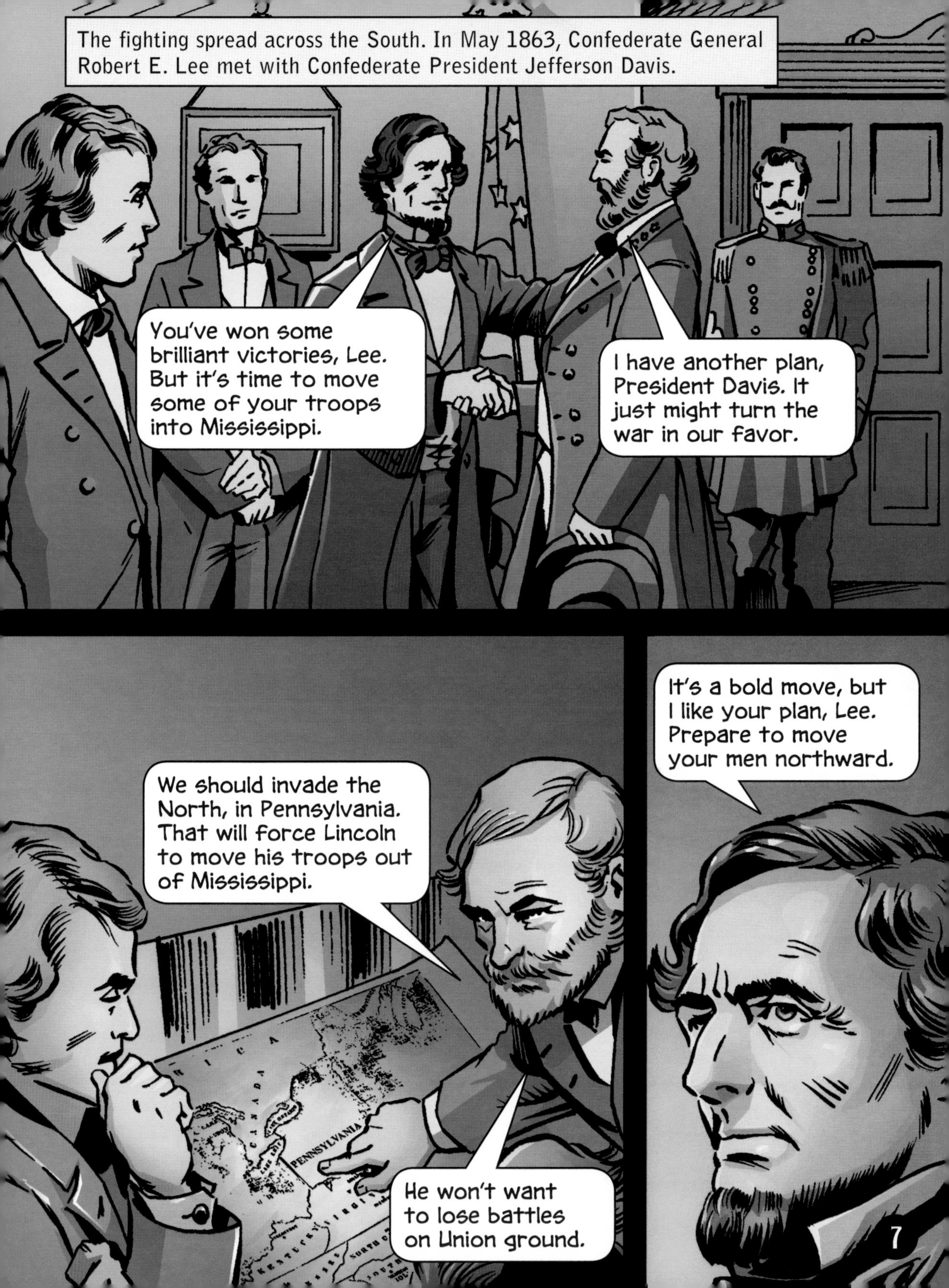
The fighting spread across the South. In May 1863, Confederate General Robert E. Lee met with Confederate President Jefferson Davis.
You've won some brilliant victories, Lee. But it's time to move some of your troops into Mississippi.
I have another plan, President Davis. It just might turn the war in our favor.
We should invade the North, in Pennsylvania. That will force Lincoln to move his troops out of Mississippi.
He won't want to lose battles on Union ground.
PENNSYLVANIA
It's a bold move, but I like your plan, Lee. Prepare to move your men northward.

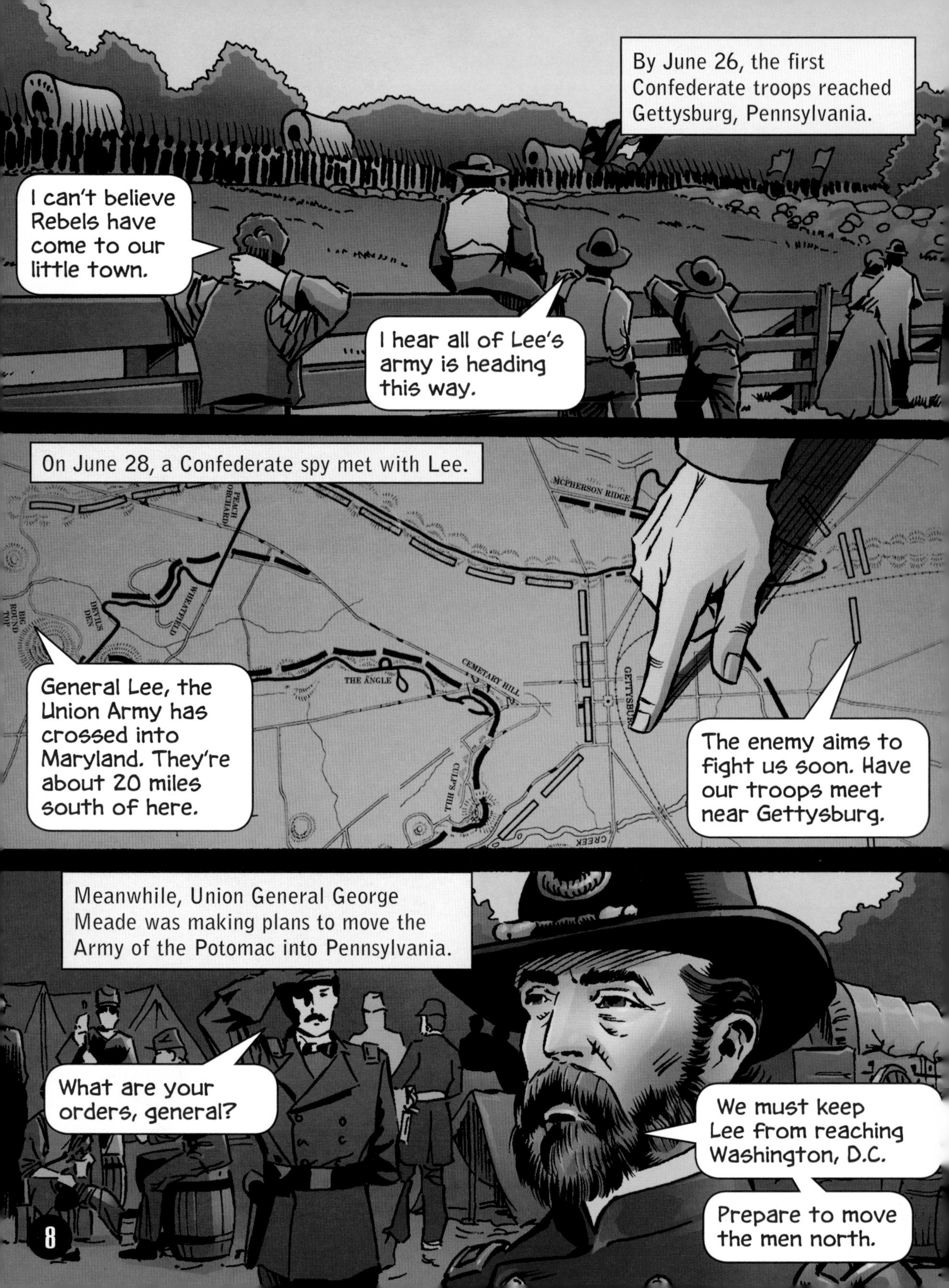
By June 26, the first Confederate troops reached Gettysburg, Pennsylvania.
I can't believe Rebels have come to our little town.
I hear all of Lee's army is heading this way.
On June 28, a Confederate spy met with Lee.
MCPHERSON RIDGE
PEACH ORCHARD
WHEATFIELD
DEVILS DEN
BIG ROUND TOP
THE ANGLE
CEMETARY HILL
CULPS HILL
General Lee, the Union Army has crossed into Maryland. They're about 20 miles south of here.
The enemy aims to fight us soon. Have our troops meet near Gettysburg.
Meanwhile, Union General George Meade was making plans to move the Army of the Potomac into Pennsylvania.
What are your orders, general?
We must keep Lee from reaching Washington, D.C.
Prepare to move the men north.

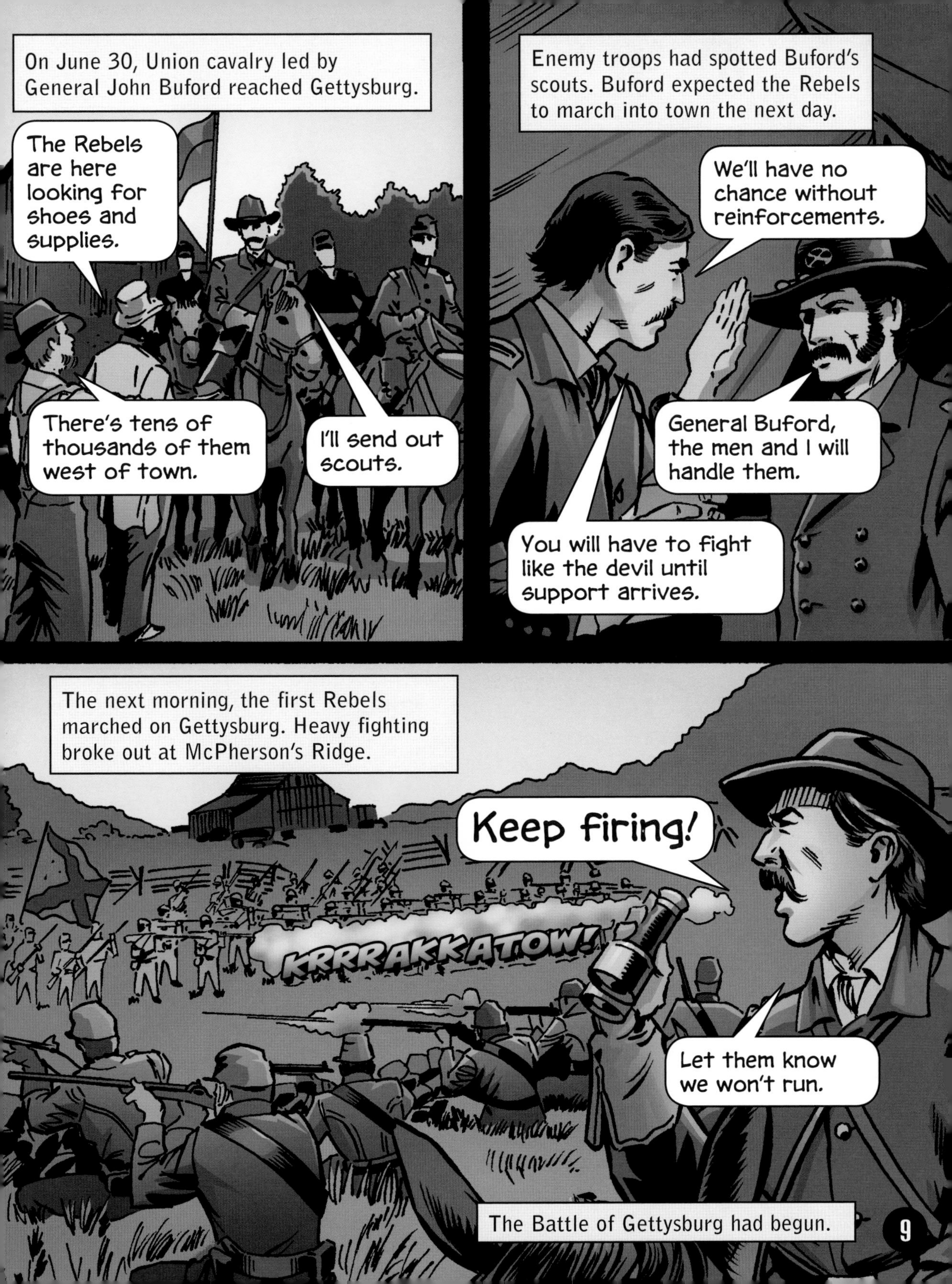

On June 30, Union cavalry led by General John Buford reached Gettysburg.
The Rebels are here looking for shoes and supplies.
There's tens of thousands of them west of town.
I'll send out scouts.
Enemy troops had spotted Buford's scouts. Buford expected the Rebels to march into town the next day.
We'll have no chance without reinforcements.
General Buford, the men and I will handle them.
You will have to fight like the devil until support arrives.
The next morning, the first Rebels marched on Gettysburg. Heavy fighting broke out at McPherson's Ridge.
Keep firing!
KRRRAKKATOW!
Let them know we won't run.
The Battle of Gettysburg had begun.

CHAPTER 2
Gains and Losses

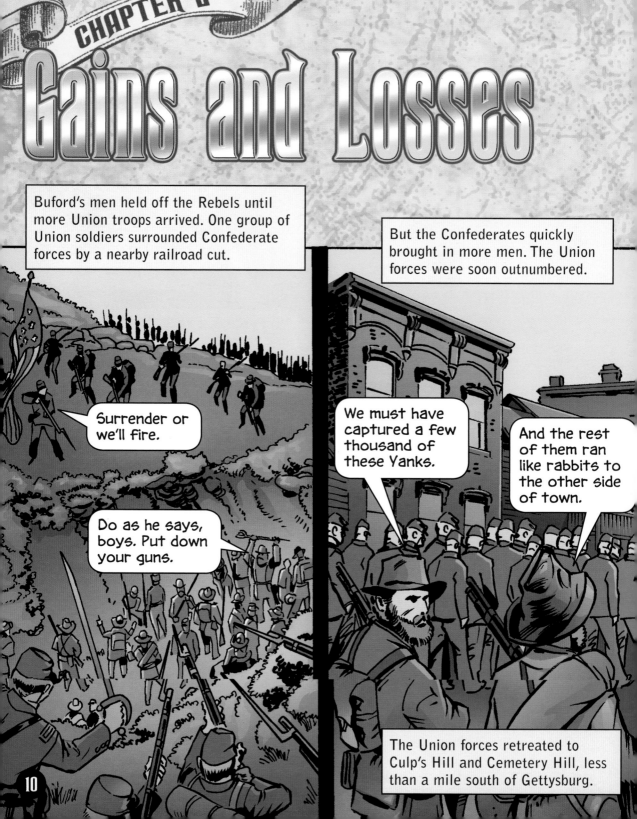

Buford's men held off the Rebels until more Union troops arrived. One group of Union soldiers surrounded Confederate forces by a nearby railroad cut.

But the Confederates quickly brought in more men. The Union forces were soon outnumbered.

Surrender or we'll fire.

We must have captured a few thousand of these Yanks.

And the rest of them ran like rabbits to the other side of town.

Do as he says, boys. Put down your guns.

The Union forces retreated to Culp's Hill and Cemetery Hill, less than a mile south of Gettysburg.

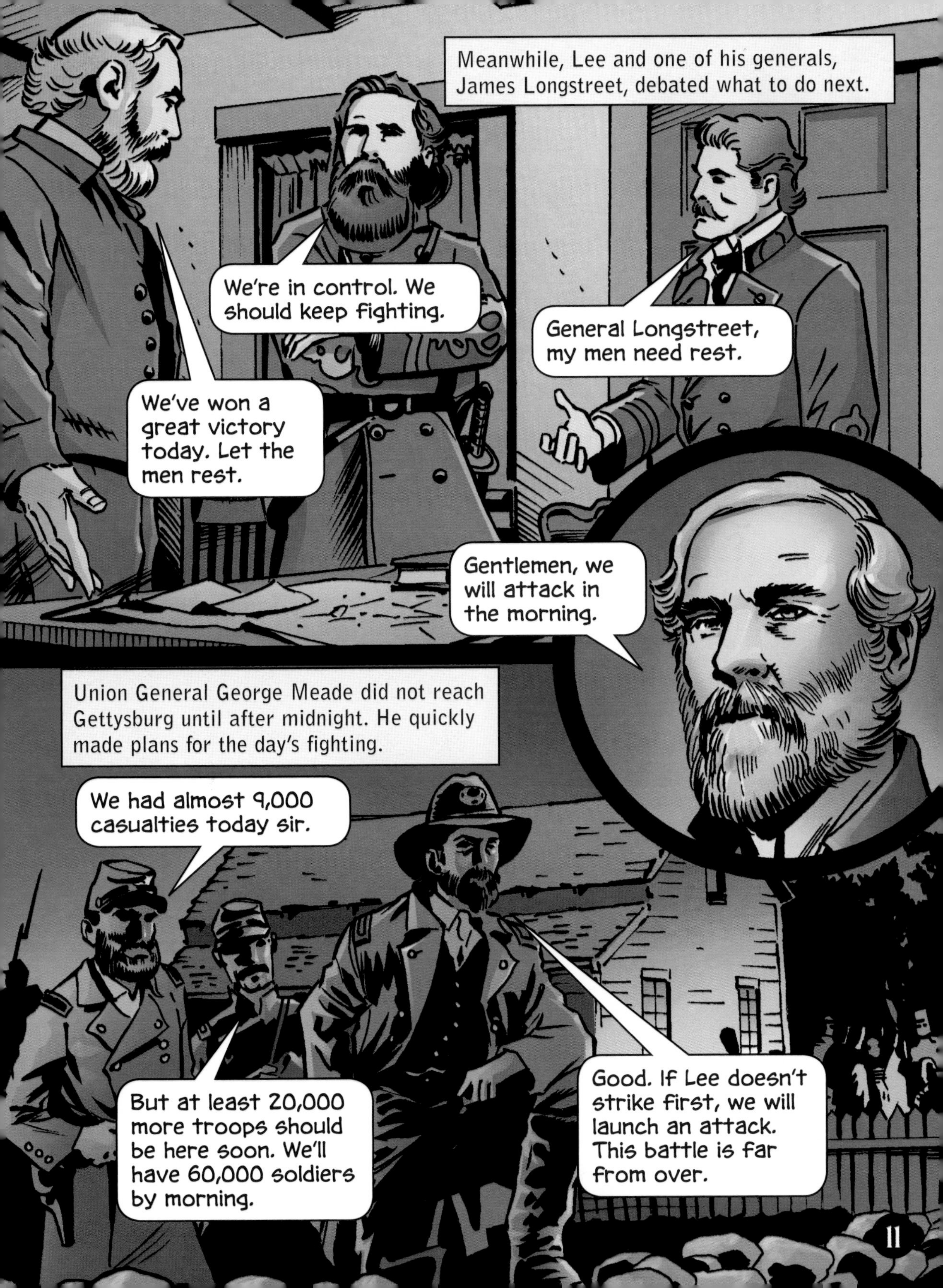
Meanwhile, Lee and one of his generals, James Longstreet, debated what to do next.
We're in control. We should keep fighting.
General Longstreet, my men need rest.
We've won a great victory today. Let the men rest.
Gentlemen, we will attack in the morning.
Union General George Meade did not reach Gettysburg until after midnight. He quickly made plans for the day's fighting.
We had almost 9,000 casualties today sir.
But at least 20,000 more troops should be here soon. We'll have 60,000 soldiers by morning.
Good. If Lee doesn't strike first, we will launch an attack. This battle is far from over.

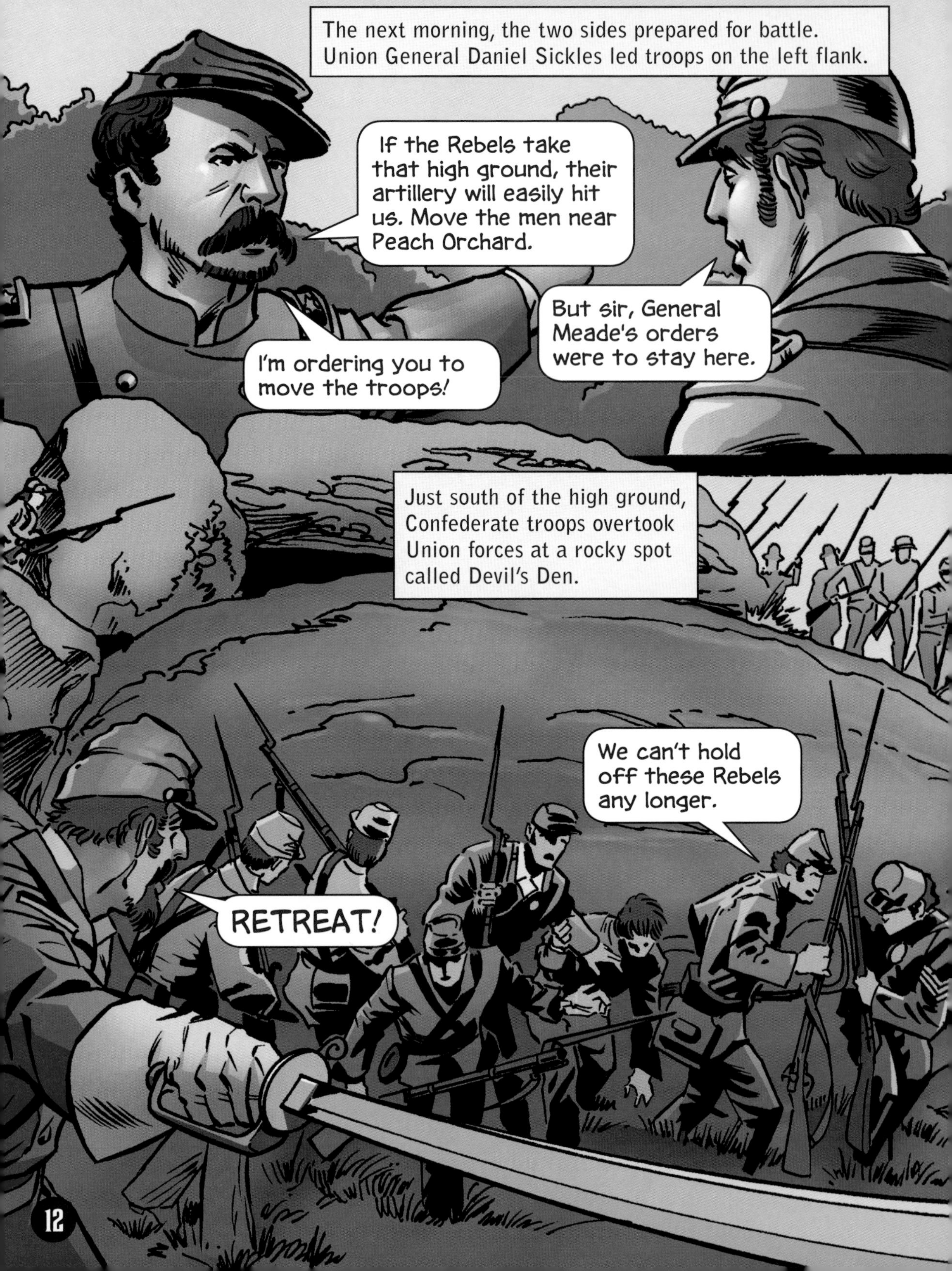

The next morning, the two sides prepared for battle. Union General Daniel Sickles led troops on the left flank.
If the Rebels take that high ground, their artillery will easily hit us. Move the men near Peach Orchard.
But sir, General Meade's orders were to stay here.
I'm ordering you to move the troops!
Just south of the high ground, Confederate troops overtook Union forces at a rocky spot called Devil's Den.
We can't hold off these Rebels any longer.
RETREAT!

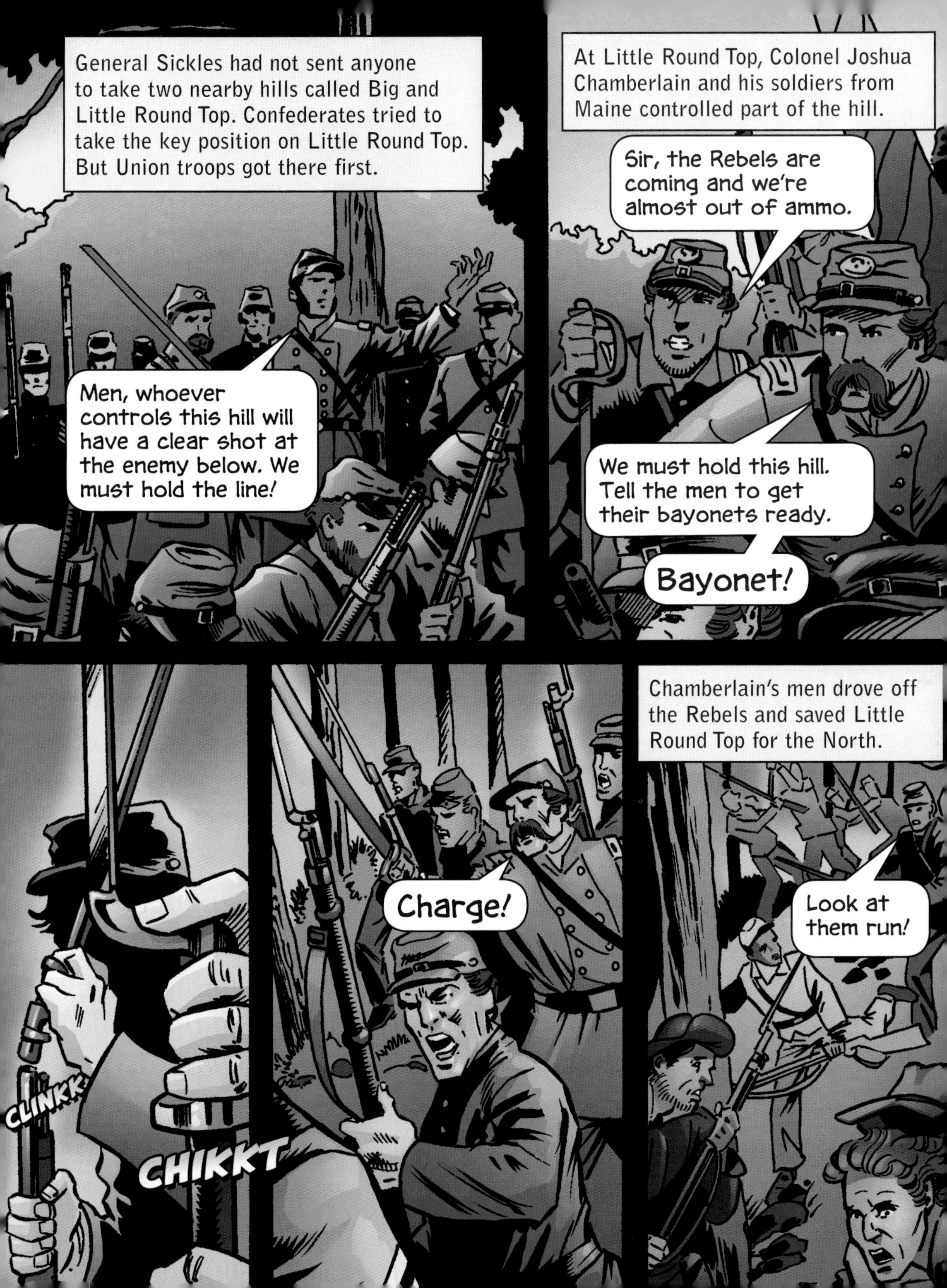
General Sickles had not sent anyone to take two nearby hills called Big and Little Round Top. Confederates tried to take the key position on Little Round Top. But Union troops got there first.
Men, whoever controls this hill will have a clear shot at the enemy below. We must hold the line!
At Little Round Top, Colonel Joshua Chamberlain and his soldiers from Maine controlled part of the hill.
Sir, the Rebels are coming and we're almost out of ammo.
We must hold this hill. Tell the men to get their bayonets ready.
Bayonet!
CLINKK
CHIKKT
Charge!
Chamberlain's men drove off the Rebels and saved Little Round Top for the North.
Look at them run!

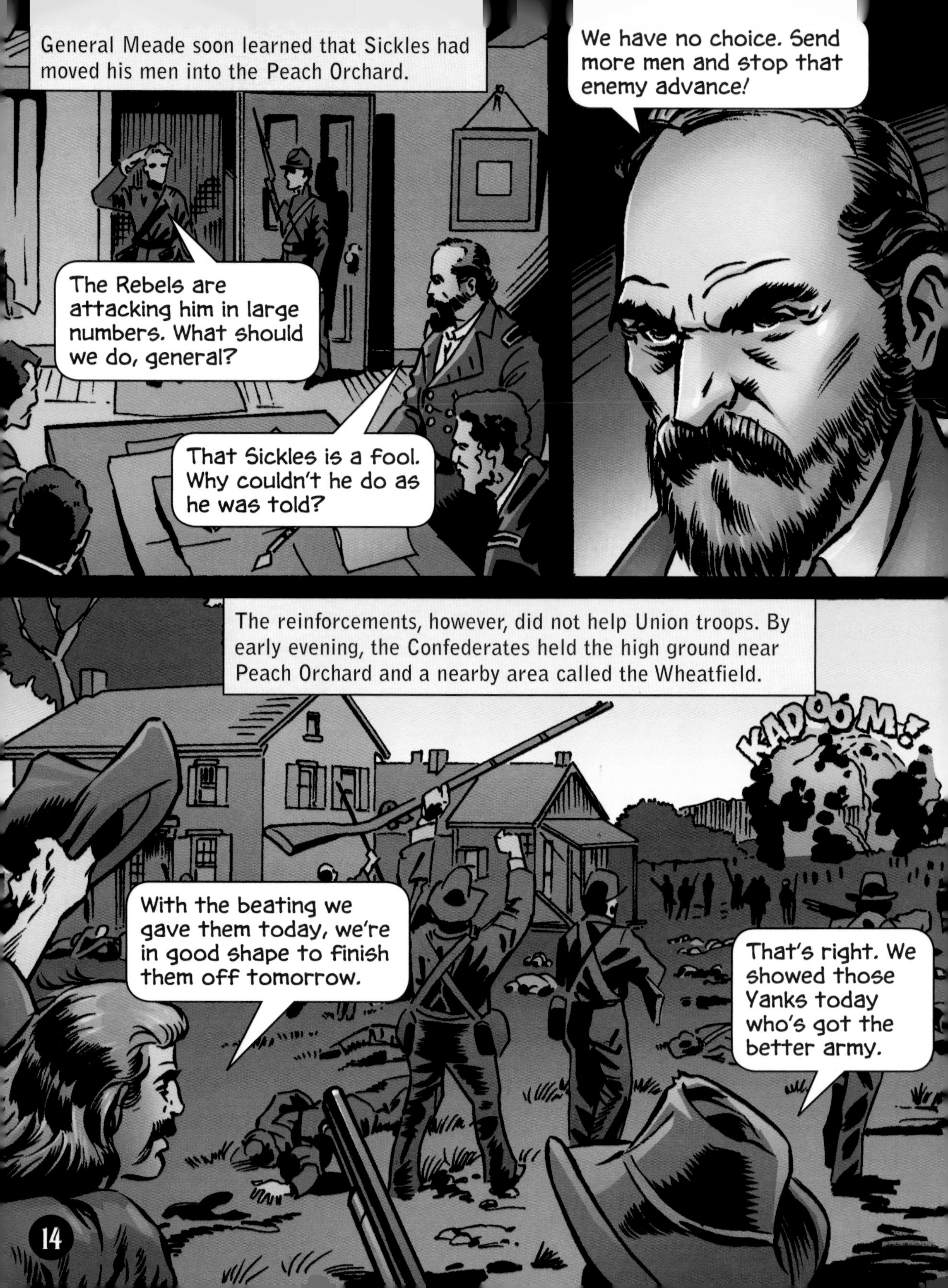

General Meade soon learned that Sickles had moved his men into the Peach Orchard.
The Rebels are attacking him in large numbers. What should we do, general?
That Sickles is a fool. Why couldn't he do as he was told?
We have no choice. Send more men and stop that enemy advance!
The reinforcements, however, did not help Union troops. By early evening, the Confederates held the high ground near Peach Orchard and a nearby area called the Wheatfield.
KADOOM!
With the beating we gave them today, we're in good shape to finish them off tomorrow.
That's right. We showed those Yanks today who's got the better army.

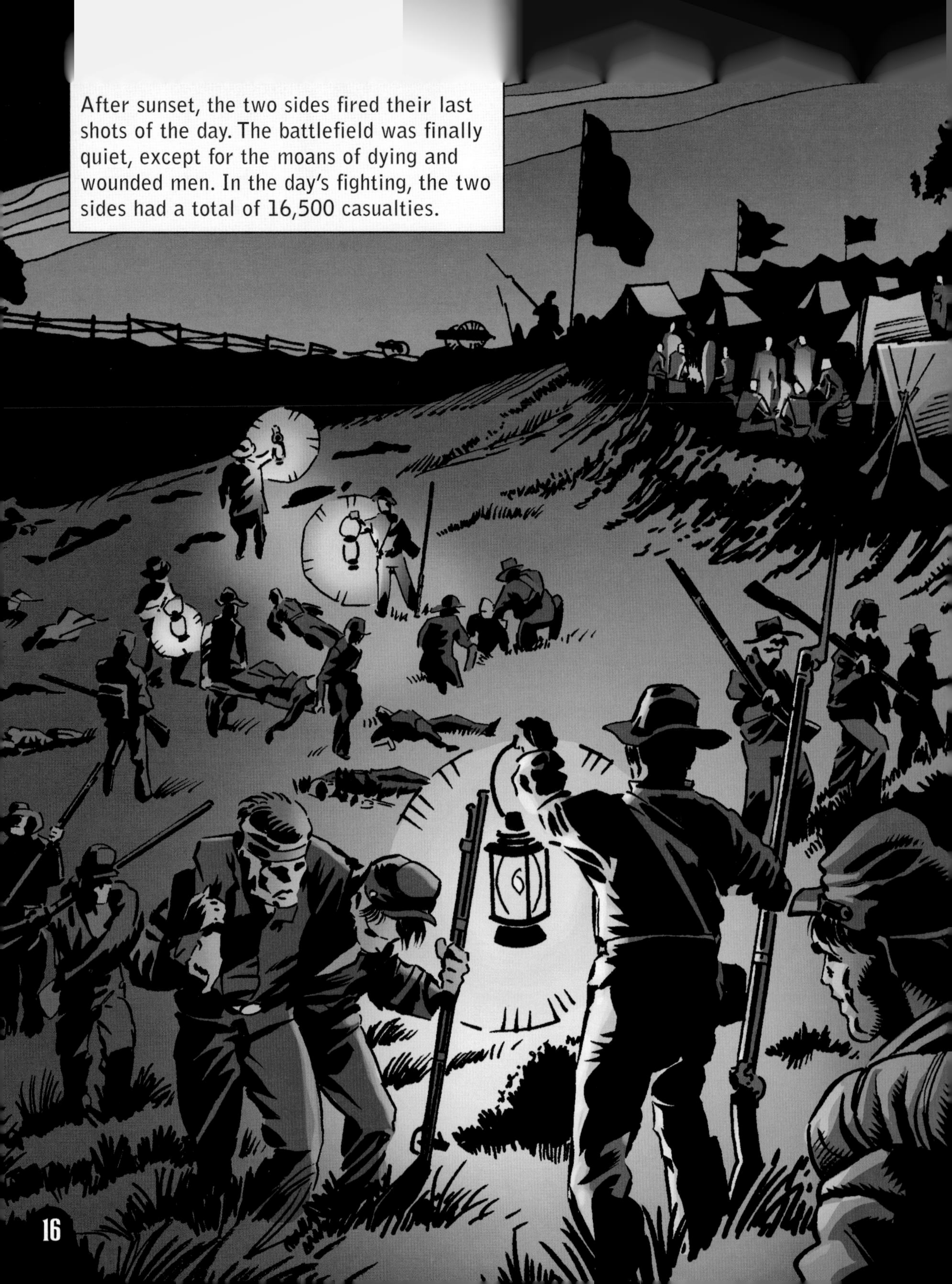
After sunset, the two sides fired their last shots of the day. The battlefield was finally quiet, except for the moans of dying and wounded men. In the day's fighting, the two sides had a total of 16,500 casualties.

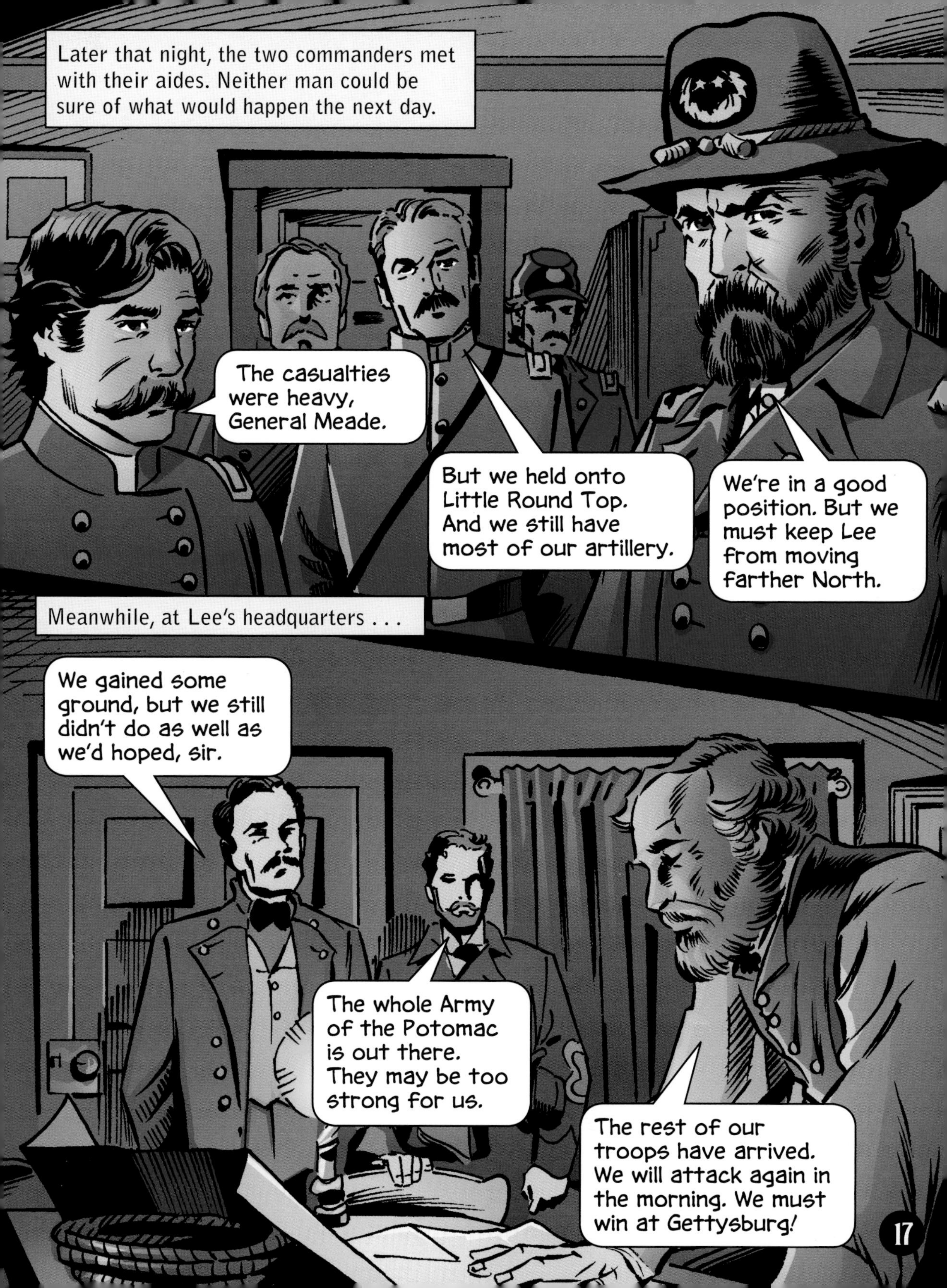
Later that night, the two commanders met with their aides. Neither man could be sure of what would happen the next day.
The casualties were heavy, General Meade.
But we held onto Little Round Top. And we still have most of our artillery.
We're in a good position. But we must keep Lee from moving farther North.
Meanwhile, at Lee's headquarters . . .
We gained some ground, but we still didn't do as well as we'd hoped, sir.
The whole Army of the Potomac is out there. They may be too strong for us.
The rest of our troops have arrived. We will attack again in the morning. We must win at Gettysburg!

CHAPTER 3
A Bloody Victory

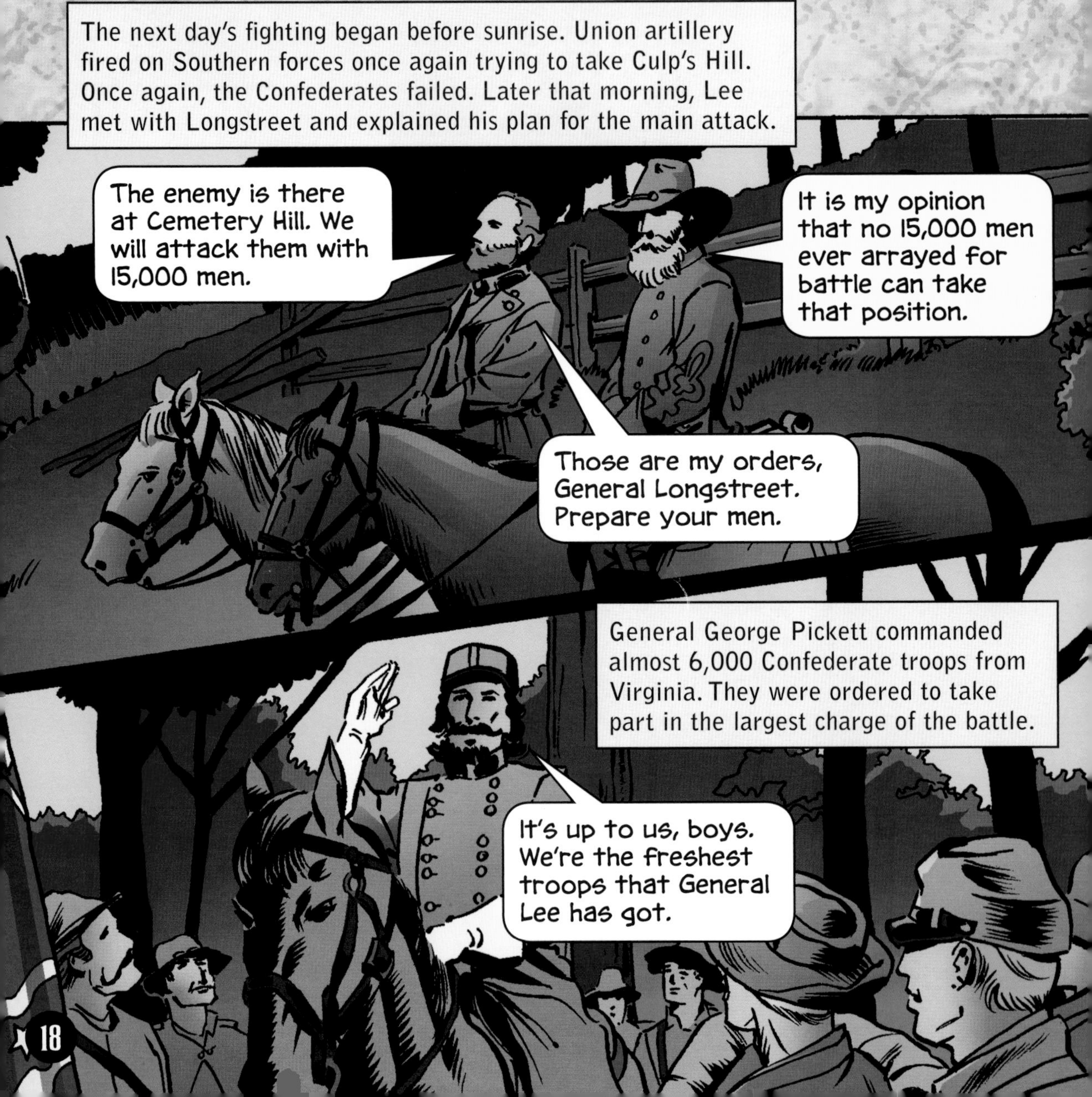
The next day's fighting began before sunrise. Union artillery fired on Southern forces once again trying to take Culp's Hill. Once again, the Confederates failed. Later that morning, Lee met with Longstreet and explained his plan for the main attack.
The enemy is there at Cemetery Hill. We will attack them with 15,000 men.
It is my opinion that no 15,000 men ever arrayed for battle can take that position.
Those are my orders, General Longstreet. Prepare your men.
General George Pickett commanded almost 6,000 Confederate troops from Virginia. They were ordered to take part in the largest charge of the battle.
It's up to us, boys. We're the freshest troops that General Lee has got.

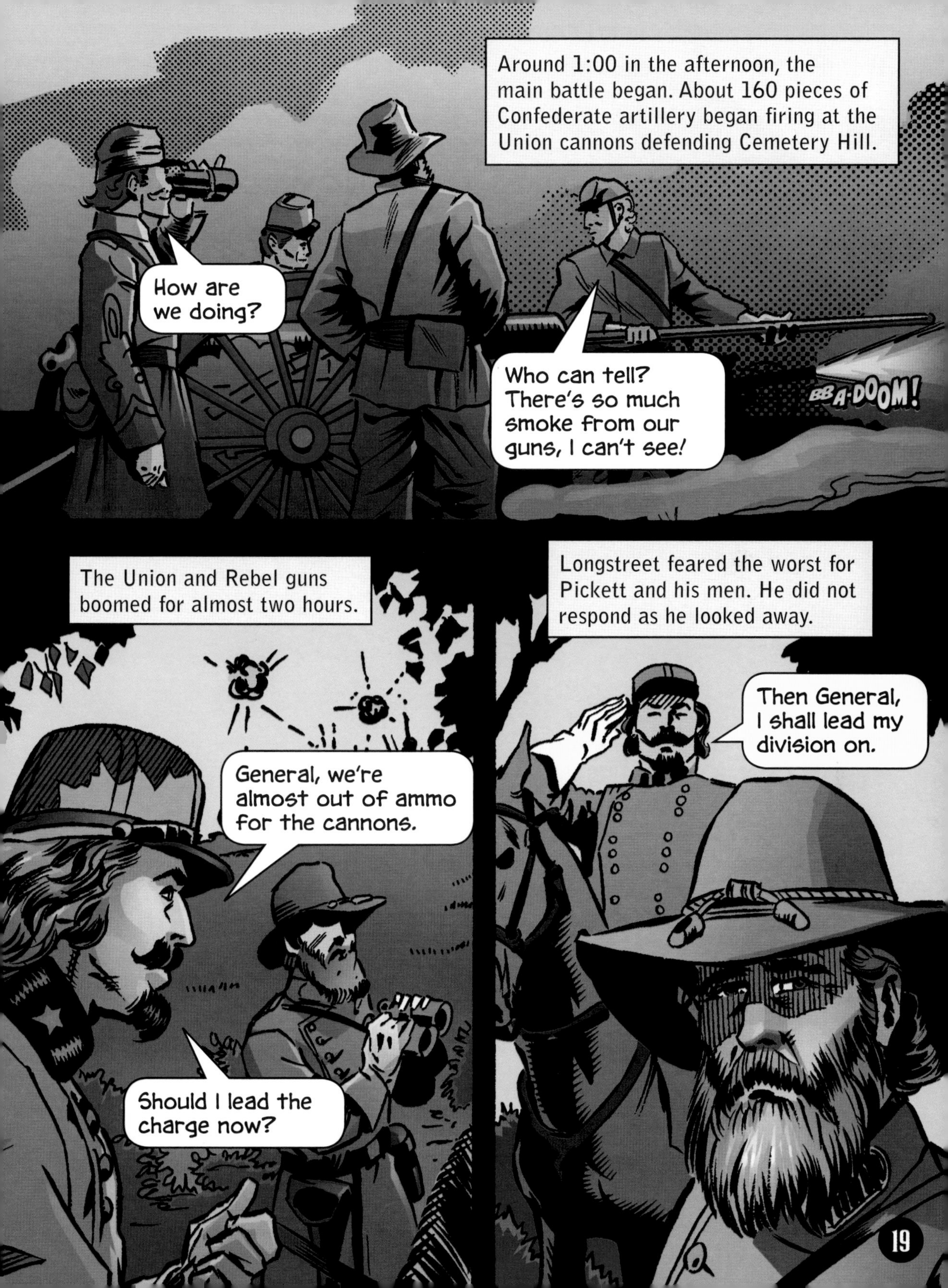
Around 1:00 in the afternoon, the main battle began. About 160 pieces of Confederate artillery began firing at the Union cannons defending Cemetery Hill.
How are we doing?
Who can tell? There's so much smoke from our guns, I can't see!
BBA-DOOM!
The Union and Rebel guns boomed for almost two hours.
General, we're almost out of ammo for the cannons.
Should I lead the charge now?
Longstreet feared the worst for Pickett and his men. He did not respond as he looked away.
Then General, I shall lead my division on.

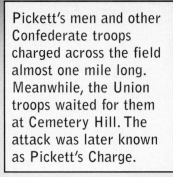

Pickett's men and other Confederate troops charged across the field almost one mile long. Meanwhile, the Union troops waited for them at Cemetery Hill. The attack was later known as Pickett's Charge.

Up men and to your posts. Don't forget today that you are from old Virginia!

WHOOM!

Stay in line, men. Keep moving forward!

The Confederates had hoped to destroy most of the Union artillery before the charge. They had failed, and now gunfire from nearby hills rained down on the Rebel troops.
KRAK!
KRAAKK!
BLAMM!
PTHOOOOM!
Get ready, boys. Here they come.

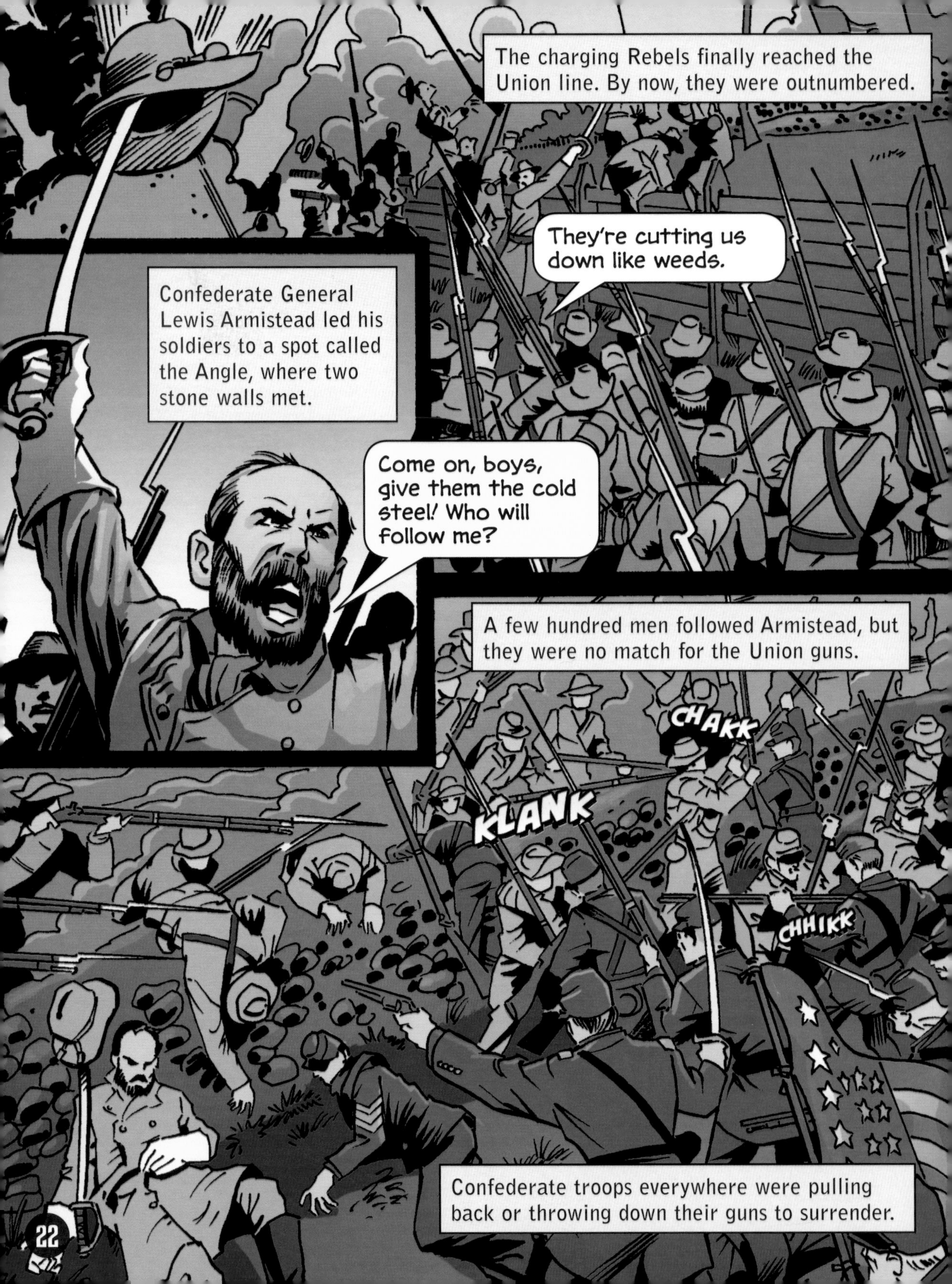
The charging Rebels finally reached the Union line. By now, they were outnumbered.
They're cutting us down like weeds.
Confederate General Lewis Armistead led his soldiers to a spot called the Angle, where two stone walls met.
Come on, boys, give them the cold steel! Who will follow me?
A few hundred men followed Armistead, but they were no match for the Union guns.
CHAKK
KLANK
CHHIKK
Confederate troops everywhere were pulling back or throwing down their guns to surrender.

CHAPTER 4

After the Battle

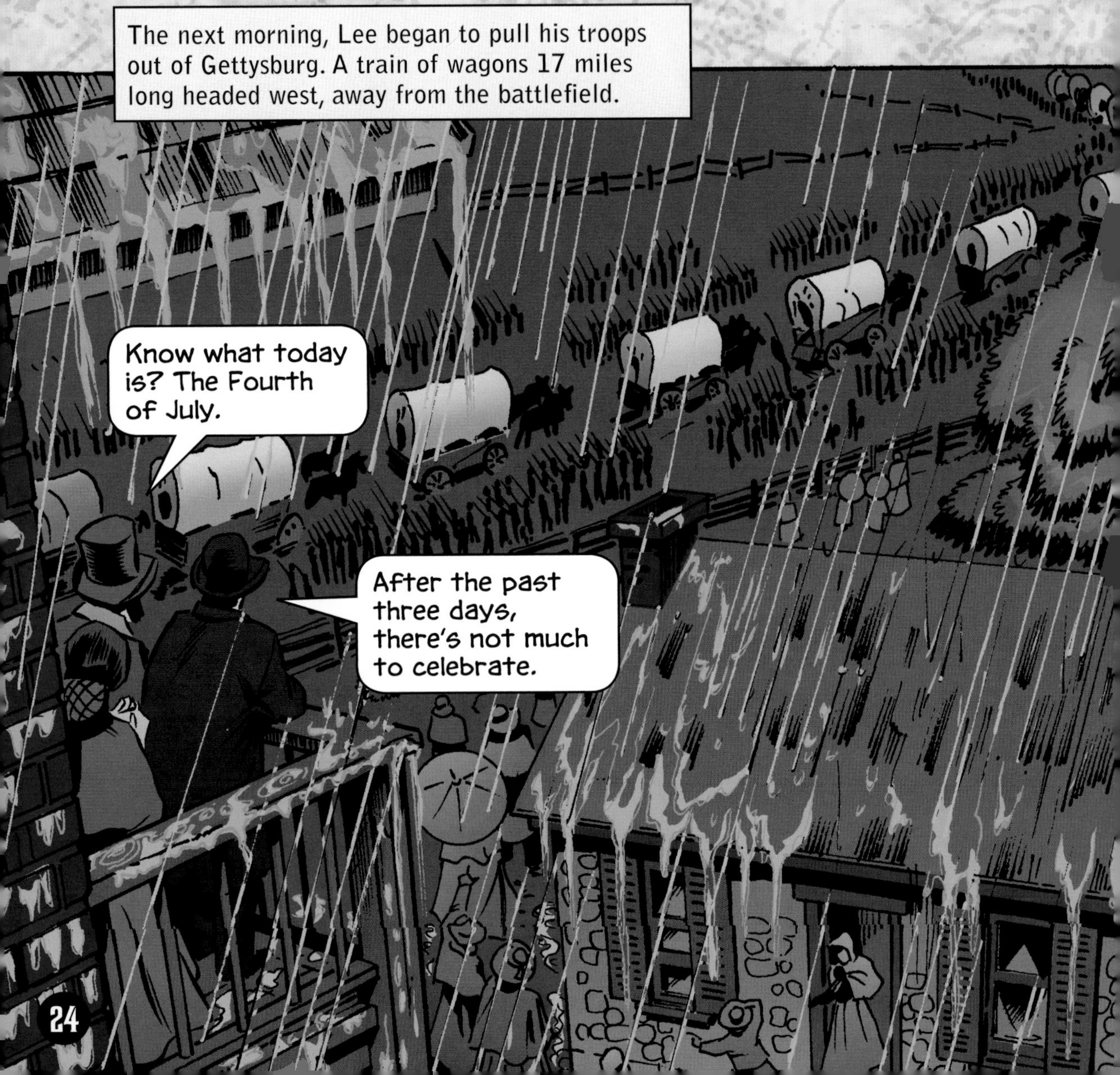

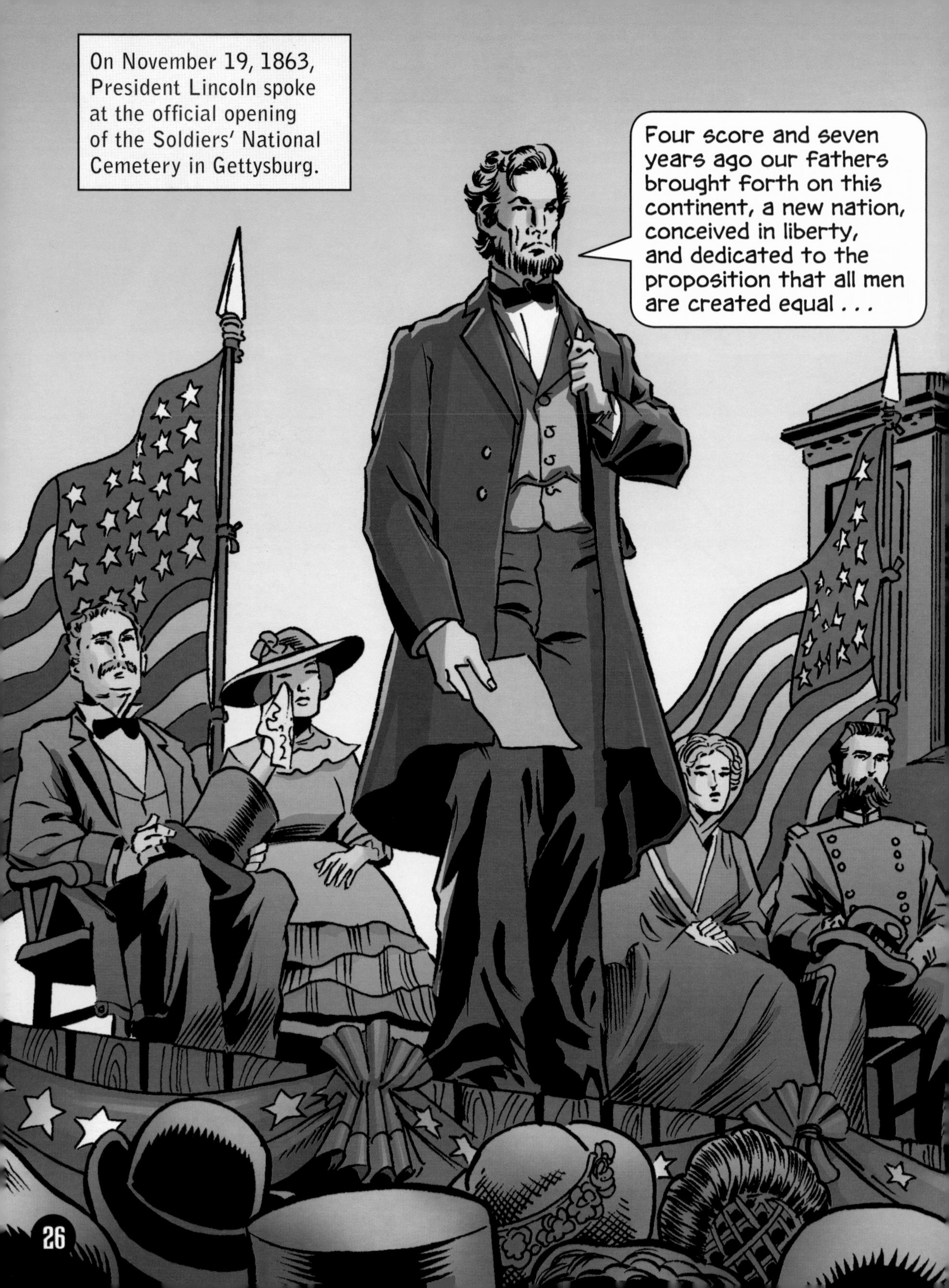
On November 19, 1863, President Lincoln spoke at the official opening of the Soldiers' National Cemetery in Gettysburg.
Four score and seven years ago our fathers brought forth on this continent, a new nation, conceived in liberty, and dedicated to the proposition that all men are created equal . . .

In his Gettysburg Address, Lincoln said that the Civil War was being fought to give all Americans freedom and equality. This speech soon became one of the most famous ever made in the United States.

After Gettysburg, the South never had the strength for another large attack on northern soil. On April 9, 1865, Lee surrendered to Union General Ulysses S. Grant near Appomattox, Virginia.

General Grant, this long and bloody war is finally over.

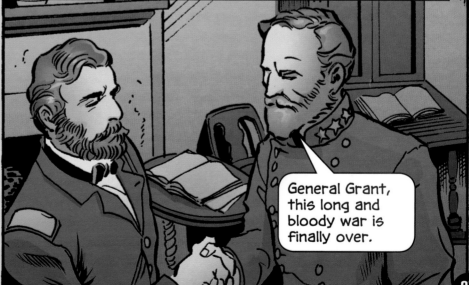

More about
The Battle of Gettysburg

The North had about 22,000 casualties at Gettysburg, out of slightly more than 93,000 troops. The South suffered about the same number of casualties out of about 70,000 troops. The combined number of casualties was the highest for any one battle of the Civil War. About another 11,000 casualties occurred in the fighting just before and after the main battle.

Abraham Lincoln personally wrote out five copies of the Gettysburg Address. Two are at the Library of Congress in Washington, D.C. One is in the White House and another is at the Abraham Lincoln Presidential Library in Springfield, Illinois. The last is at Cornell University in New York.

About 3,500 Union soldiers are buried at the Soldiers' National Cemetery in Gettysburg.

In 1895, the U.S. government created Gettysburg National Military Park. The park includes the cemetery and the battlefield around it. Today, the park covers nearly 6,000 acres and has 26 miles of roads. At least 1.8 million people visit the park each year.

The Gettysburg Address

Four score and seven years ago our fathers brought forth, upon this continent, a new nation, conceived in Liberty, and dedicated to the proposition that all men are created equal.

Now we are engaged in a great civil war, testing whether that nation, or any nation, so conceived, and so dedicated, can long endure. We are met here on a great battlefield of that war. We have come to dedicate a portion of it as a final resting place for those who here gave their lives that that nation might live. It is altogether fitting and proper that we should do this.

But in a larger sense we can not dedicate-we can not consecrate-we can not hallow this ground. The brave men, living and dead, who struggled, here, have consecrated it far above our poor power to add or detract. The world will little note, nor long remember, what we say here, but can never forget what they did here. It is for us, the living, rather to be dedicated here to the unfinished work which they have, thus far, so nobly carried on. It is rather for us to be here dedicated to the great task remaining before us-that from these honored dead we take increased devotion to that cause for which they here gave the last full measure of devotion-that we here highly resolve that these dead shall not have died in vain; that this nation shall have a new birth of freedom; and that this government of the people, by the people, for the people, shall not perish from the earth.

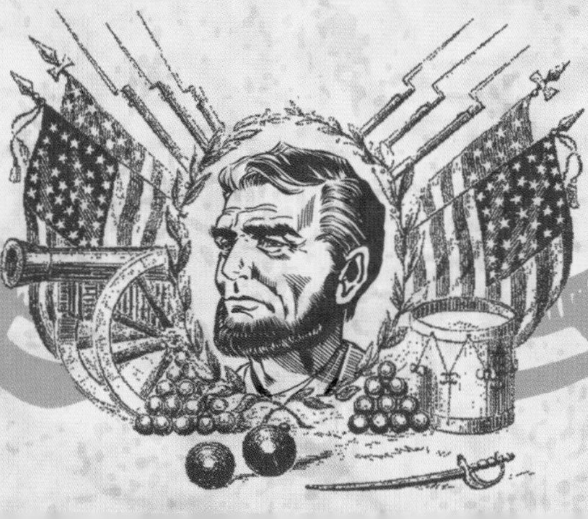

GLOSSARY

ammunition (am-yuh-NISH-uhn)—bullets and other objects that can be fired from weapons; ammunition is called "ammo" for short.

artillery (ar-TIL-uh-ree)—large, powerful guns

casualties (KAZH-oo-uhl-tees)—soldiers killed, wounded, captured, or reported missing after a battle

corps (KOR)—a group of military officers and enlisted members

counterattack (KOUN-ter-uh-tak)—fighting begun by one side after it has slowed or stopped an enemy's original attack

flank (FLANGK)—area to the side of a group of soldiers

INTERNET SITES

FactHound offers a safe, fun way to find Internet sites related to this book. All of the sites on FactHound have been researched by our staff.

Here's how:

1. *Visit www.facthound.com*
2. Type in this special code **0736854916** for age-appropriate sites. Or enter a search word related to this book for a more general search.
3. Click on the **Fetch It** button.

FactHound will fetch the best sites for you!

READ MORE

Anderson, Dale. *The Battle of Gettysburg.* Landmark Events in American History. Milwaukee: World Almanac Library, 2003.

McPherson, James M. *Fields of Fury: The American Civil War.* New York: Atheneum Books for Young Readers, 2002.

Stone, Tanya Lee. *Abraham Lincoln.* DK Biography. New York: DK Publishing, 2005.

Tanaka, Shelley. *Gettysburg.* A Day that Changed America. New York: Hyperion Books for Children, 2003.

BIBLIOGRAPHY

Catton, Bruce. *The American Heritage New History of the Civil War.* New York: Viking, 1996.

Johnston, David Emmons. *The Story of a Confederate Boy in the Civil War.* Portland, Ore.: Glass & Prudhomme, 1914.

Sears, Stephen W. *Gettysburg.* Boston: Houghton Mifflin, 2003.

Tagg, Larry. *The Generals of Gettysburg: The Leaders of America's Greatest Battle.* Campbell, Calif.: Savas Publishing, 1998.

INDEX